YOUR KNOWLEDGE HAS VALUE

- We will publish your bachelor's and master's thesis, essays and papers

- Your own eBook and book - sold worldwide in all relevant shops

- Earn money with each sale

Upload your text at www.GRIN.com and publish for free

Bibliographic information published by the German National Library:

The German National Library lists this publication in the National Bibliography; detailed bibliographic data are available on the Internet at http://dnb.dnb.de .

Imprint:

Copyright © 2015 GRIN Verlag, Open Publishing GmbH
Print and binding: Books on Demand GmbH, Norderstedt Germany
ISBN: 978-3-668-07287-9

This book at GRIN:

http://www.grin.com/en/e-book/308395/study-on-the-mental-health-status-of-adolescents-studying-in-the-secondary

Nivedita Bezbaruah

Study on the Mental Health Status of Adolescents Studying in the Secondary Schools of Jorhat District, Assam

GRIN Publishing

Study on the Mental Health Status of Adolescents Studying in the Secondary Schools of Jorhat District, Assam.

Nivedita Bezbaruah

ABSTRACT

In the present study an attempt was made to study the mental health status of adolescents belonging to the Jorhat district of Assam .The sample of 500 adolescents (250 male and 250 female) were taken from various schools of Jorhat district. Tools used for the study was the Mental Health Battery developed by Dr. Arun Kumar Singh and Dr. Alpana Sengupta . Results clearly indicated that majority of the adolescents have average mental health and no significant difference was found in the adolescent boys and girls studying in the Secondary schools of Jorhat district.

Key Words: Mental Health Status, Adolescents, Secondary Schools.

Introduction:

Mental Health represents the degree of good or normal functioning. It includes an individual's ability to enjoy life and procure a balance between life activities and efforts to achieve psychological resilience. World Health Organization defines mental health as "*a state of well being in which the individual realizes his/her own abilities, can cope with the normal stresses of life, can work productively and fruitfully, and is able to make a contribution to his or her community*". The importance of maintaining good mental health is crucial to living a long and healthy life. Good mental health can enhance one's life, while poor mental health can prevent someone from living a normal life. A person possessing sound mental health can adjust well to the environmental situations and inter personal relations. Such a person has a clear self-concept, accepts his limitations and does not blame others for his deficiencies. He develops tension-tolerance and does not get disturbed in moment of distress.

** Research Scholar, Department of Education, Dibrugarh University, Dibrugarh, Assam*

Sutherland et al.,(1953) reported that the joint goal of all types of education is mental health. It aims at developing the growth of both intellectual and emotional potentialities of an individual in an intricate and complex culture.

Need and significance of the Study:

Today much importance is being given to mental health and related areas because it has been found that a poor mental health condition may prevent an individual from doing any progressive activity. Mental health is the foundation for well being and effective functioning for an individual and for a community.

The foremost concern of education today is to produce mentally healthy persons who are well-adjusted personalities, because mentally healthy persons are the real assets of the society for the 21st century. When something shocking happens, attention is immediately focused on the need for doing something about mental health. Thus for the development of the society, mental hygiene is very much essential to the children which in turn can maintain balanced mental health. Thus the mental health of the students is the most important topic of the day as they are the future assets of our society. Mental health is now recognized as important and is an integral part of our life as, a mentally healthy person is one who is happy, lives peacefully with his neighbours, makes his children healthy citizens and after fulfilling such basic responsibilities is still empowered with sufficient strength to serve the cause of the society in any way.

Objectives of the study:

- ➢ To find out the mental health status of the adolescents studying in the secondary schools of Jorhat district, Assam.
- ➢ To compare the mental health status of adolescents studying in the secondary schools of Jorhat district, Assam, with reference to gender.
- ➢ To compare the mental health status of adolescents studying in the secondary schools of

  Jorhat district, Assam in relation to the different dimensions of mental health, with reference to gender.

Hypotheses of the study:

Keeping in view the objectives mentioned above, the following hypotheses were specified in null form, as shown below:

- There is no significant difference in the mental health status among the adolescent boys and girls studying in the secondary schools of Jorhat district, Assam.

- There is no significant dimension-wise difference in the mental health status of the adolescent boys and girls studying in the Secondary schools of Jorhat district, Assam.

Operational Definitions of the Terms Used:

a) **Mental Health Status :-** Mental Health is a state of the individual in which he/she is able to perform at his/her optimal level, with a minimum of tension and friction and a maximum of happiness, efficiency to themselves and to the world at large, while also being able to contribute to society. Status refers to a state/condition of mind. In the present study, the term mental health status would mean the condition of the mind wherein it functions at an optimal level with reference to the dimensions of the Mental Health Battery (*that has been used as the tool to assess the mental health status*), **viz., emotional stability, overall adjustment, autonomy, security-insecurity, self-concept and intelligence**.

b) **Adolescents:-** Chronologically the period of adolescence comes roughly in between the years from 12 to 20. In the present study, the operational definition of the term *'adolescents'* refers to the students of Class IX in the Secondary schools of Jorhat district.

c) **Secondary Schools:-** In the present study, secondary schools will be used to mean all those schools within Jorhat district which have secondary education classes from Class VI up to Class X (at least). Since the target population sample were from Classes IX (who will be followed up till Class X), those schools which may not have the higher secondary sections within its fold will also be taken up as the proposed sample of study.

Methodology of the Study:

In the present study "Survey Method " or " Normative Survey Method" was used .

Population and sample:

The population of the present study comprised of all the pupils of Class IX studying in Secondary schools of Jorhat district . To conduct the study, 500 students of Class IX (250 Male & 250 Female), studying in the Secondary schools of Jorhat district were selected as the sample for the present study. The researcher selected 20 secondary schools using purposive sampling technique and students from each school was selected by means of quota sampling technique.

Tool used for the study:

The tool used for collection of data was a standardized **"Mental Health Battery"** prepared by Dr. Arun Kumar Singh, Professor, Dept. of Psychology, Patna University, Patna and Dr Alpana Sengupta, Lecturer, Dept. of Psychology, College of Commerce, Patna. It intends to assess the mental health status of persons in the age range of 13 to 22 yrs. Mental Health Battery consists of 130 items divided into six parts (*Emotional Stability, Over all adjustment, Autonomy, Security-Insecurity, self concept and intelligence*)

Analytical Procedure:

Statistical techniques like Mean, Standard Deviation, t test and Percentiles, were used in the analysis of data. In order to compare the mental health status among the adolescent boys and girls studying in the secondary schools of Jorhat district, the' t' test was used. To find out the mental health status of the adolescents a five point qualitative criterion on the basis of socio –economic status was used to classify sample with respect to their mental health.

Analysis of the Findings of the Study:

The findings of the study are discussed below according to the objectives of the study and the hypotheses framed with regard to each objective. These are presented below serially:

Mental health status of the Adolescents studying in the Secondary Schools of Jorhat district, Assam: The findings of the Mental Health Battery that was used to test the mental health status of the student sample from the secondary schools of Jorhat selected, have been presented as percentile scores, as per directions for scoring of the scores against each question in the Battery used for this study. These are presented in **Table No.-1** given below:

Table No. – 1

*Mental Health Status of the Adolescents studying
in the Secondary Schools of Jorhat district, Assam.*

Percentile	No of Adolescents			Total	Category
	SES(High)	SES(Middle)	SES(Low)		
P_{90} and above	21	1	0	22	Excellent Mental Health
P_{70} to P_{90}	9	26	17	52	Good Mental Health
P_{50} to P_{70}	55	87	35	177	Average Mental Health
P_{30} to P_{50}	24	49	30	103	Poor Mental Health
Below P_{30}	21	67	58	146	Very poor Mental Health
Total	130	230	140	500	

From the percentile scores of the **Table No. 1**, given above, it is clear that the majority of the students (177) from the 500 sampled students have <u>average mental health</u>; and the next highest number of students (146) fall within the percentile P_{30} to P_{50} which indicates <u>very poor mental health</u>. Only 22 students out of the total 500 were in the range of the highest percentile indicator of <u>excellent mental health</u>. Majority of the sampled students fell in the categories of average, poor and very poor mental health.

Comparison of the Mental Health Status of Adolescents studying in the Secondary Schools of Jorhat district, Assam with reference to Gender : <u>Table No. 2</u>, given below, shows the comparison of the mental health status of adolescents studying in the secondary schools of Jorhat district, Assam with reference to their gender.

Table No. – 2

*Comparison of Mental Health Status among Adolescents Boys and Girls studying in the
Secondary Schools of Jorhat district:*

Sex	N	Mean	SD	't' value	Significance
Boys	250	81.04	19.66	0.20	Not Significant at 0.05 level.
Girls	250	80.68	19.52		

5

From **Table – 2**, it is evident that <u>the 't' value was found to be 0.20 which is less than 1.96 and therefore not significant at 0.05 level.</u> *So, the null hypothesis which mentioned that there is no significant difference in the mental health status of secondary school adolescents of Jorhat district, Assam, with reference to their gender is accepted.* **In other words, the findings of the sample studied helps in forming the conclusion that there is no significant difference in the mental health status among the adolescent boys and girls in the secondary schools of Jorhat.**

Comparison of the Mental Health Status of Adolescents boys and girls studying in the Secondary Schools of Jorhat district, Assam, in relation to the different dimensions of Mental Health defined in the Mental Health Battery : The findings in this regard are shown in the **Table No. – 3** given below:

Table No. - 3

***Comparison of the Mental Health Status of Adolescent Boys and Girls
in relation to the different Dimensions of Mental Health.***

Sl No	Dimension	Mental Health						
		N	Boys		Girls		't' value	Significance
			Mean	SD	Mean	SD		
I	Emotional Stability	250	8.17	1.82	7.71	2.76	2.3	Significant at 0.05 level.
II	Over all Adjustment	250	24.98	6.43	24.40	6.65	1	Not Significant at 0.05 level
III	Autonomy	250	10.24	2.63	10.09	2.69	0.67	Not Significant at 0.05 level.
IV	Security Insecurity	250	8.62	2.53	8.49	2.61	0.57	Not Significant at 0.05 level.
V	Self concept	250	9.61	3.07	9.6	2.97	0.03	Not Significant at 0.05 level.
VI	Intelligence	250	19.58	5.93	19.20	5.38	0.76	Not Significant at 0.05 level.

From the scores given in **Table No. -3,** it is observed that the calculated 't' value for the dimensions *overall adjustment, autonomy, security insecurity, self concept and intelligence* are 1, 0.67, 0.57, 0.03, 0.76 which are less than critical value of 't'(1.96) and therefore not significant at 0.05 level of significance. Hence, the conclusion is that there is a no significant difference in the dimension *of **overall adjustment, autonomy, security insecurity, self concept and intelligence*** among the adolescent boys and girls in the secondary schools of Jorhat district .On the other hand the calculated 't' value for the dimension *emotional stability* is 2.3 which is greater than critical value of 't'(1.96) and therefore significant at 0.05 level of significance. Hence, the conclusion is that there is significant difference in the dimension of ***emotional stability*** among the adolescent boys and girls in the secondary schools of Jorhat district.

Thus, on the basis of the findings given above, with regard to the six dimensions of the Mental Health Battery, the conclusion drawn was that except for the first dimension of the scale, i.e., *emotional stability,* where there was a significant difference among the adolescent boys and girls in respect of this aspect of mental health status, there were no significant differences among the sampled adolescents studying in the Secondary schools of Jorhat district, with respect to the rest of the five dimensions of the standardized tool used to assess mental health of these students.   Therefore, the null hypothesis that stated that *there is no significant dimension-wise difference in the mental health status of the adolescent boys and girls studying in the secondary schools of Jorhat district, Assam,* may be only partially accepted as valid for five out of six dimensions of mental health status scale, *viz., overall adjustment, autonomy, security-insecurity, self-concept and intelligence*, and rejected for the first dimension of the same, *i.e., emotional stability.*

Discussion

On the basis of the over all analysis shown in the different tables given above, the following major interpretations may be made of the findings of the present study.

i.   The findings of the present study indicate that Adolescents of higher socio-economic status were found to be comparatively more in numbers in the domain of excellent mental health which may be an indicator that socio-economic status also can affect one's mental health. The adolescents of higher socio-economic status usually get better facilities in all aspects in comparison to the adolescents belonging to the lower socio- economic status. The findings indicated that more than half of the adolescents fell in the category of average, poor and very poor mental health. The reasons for this might be due to poverty, social inequality, poor nutrition, dysfunctional home life as well as lack of awareness of the factors which facilitate mental health. Moreover, poor health-care services (both physical and mental) might also be one of the causes of average and poor mental health.

ii.   Mental health status of adolescent boys and girls studying in the Secondary Schools of Jorhat district <u>do not differ significantly</u>. This might be due to the reason that the nowadays males and females are treated as equals in almost all respect and also given equal facilities in almost all areas, especially regarding education, family encouragement, participation in all activities, visiting different places etc. Educational empowerment especially, seems to be a major equalizer of the gendered constructs generally prevailing in society. Mental health status of adolescent boys and girls <u>differ significantly</u> in relation to the dimensions of ***emotional stability*** .Mental health status of adolescent boys and girls <u>do not differ significantly</u> in relation to the dimensions of ***overall adjustment, autonomy, security-insecurity, self-concept and intelligence.***

Educational Implications:

i.   The present study revealed that a majority of the adolescents were found to have average and poor mental health. Thus all school and community projects should be planned in such a way as to encourage the promotion of mental health amongst students. The society should be made aware that child-rearing practices should be improved upon in such a way that children have close and understanding relationships with their parents and other adults around them. This will reduce mental health problems and lead to an improved social and economic status of the individual and the nation.

ii. The home and school should take steps to keep the adolescents mentally and emotionally healthy. Along with exercise and healthy nutritionally-balanced foods to prevent physical ailments, it's important to also incorporate relaxation and stress-relief techniques into their daily lives so as to prevent mental and emotional distress. They should be taught about the benefits of deep-breathing exercises, meditation, and many other strategies that enhance mental health and both the school and the home can ensure that these are practiced by the young adolescents.

Conclusion:

In the present study, an attempt was made by the researcher to study the mental health status of today's adolescents with the help of a standardized Mental Health Status Battery. From the findings, it was realized that majority of the adolescents (177 nos.) from the 500 sampled students of Jorhat district have <u>average mental health</u>; and the next highest number of students (146 Nos) also have scores which indicate <u>very poor mental health</u>. Only 22 students out of the total 500 were in the range of the highest percentile indicator of <u>excellent mental health</u>. Majority of the sampled students fell in the categories of average, poor and very poor mental health status. These findings need further analysis regarding the possible causes for the poor mental health status of these youngsters. Adolescents of higher socio-economic status were found to be comparatively more in numbers in the domain of excellent mental health which may be an indicator that socio –economic status also can affect one's mental health. Other research studies in this area have also reflected the same trend, and thus such a finding is true not only in Jorhat district, but also in other parts of India. All these seem to indicate that there is a widening chasm of differences between the school adolescents of today who are exposed to more varied sources of information and education nowadays than during earlier times. Their exposure to various means of mass media seems to be threatening to break the thin veneer of social control at home, school or in society. Moreover, the decreasing trends of values in today's generation, is also a matter of increasing concern. The needs of today's adolescents need to be addressed urgently by society through guidance and counseling, along with value education at all levels. Thus, one may safely conclude by saying that it now becomes the responsibility of governance to undertake certain urgent policy decisions to bring about such positive and dynamic changes in teaching-learning situations.

References:

1. **Sutherland et al.(1953).** Survey of Mental Health of Foreign Students. *Scandinavian Journal of Psychology,*32,(1), 22-30.

2. **World Health Organisation.(2005).** Promoting Mental Health: Concepts, Emerging evidence, Practice: A report of the World Health Organisation, Department of Mental Health and Substance Abuse in collaboration with the Victorian Health Promotion Foundation and the University of Melbourne . World Health Organisation. Geneva.

****

YOUR KNOWLEDGE HAS VALUE

- We will publish your bachelor's and
  master's thesis, essays and papers

- Your own eBook and book -
  sold worldwide in all relevant shops

- Earn money with each sale

Upload your text at www.GRIN.com
and publish for free